HOME COMPUTER SECURITY

ON THE CHEAP

A simple and inexpensive approach to keeping things secure at home.

By Lance Jeffery, CCNA,

CCNA Security

Table of Contents

INTRODUCTION..1

RULE NUMBER 1
Secure Your Border...4

RULE NUMBER 2
Secure Your Network...13

RULE NUMBER 3
Secure Your PC..17

RULE NUMBER 4
Secure Your Mobile Devices...29

RULE NUMBER 5
Stay Vigilant..32

APPENDIX 37

GLOSSARY...39

INTRODUCTION

I have worked in IT for nearly 15 years and during my tenure as an IT Geek, I have worked for a Credit Union, a Marketing firm, a Computer Software firm and a Manufacturing firm. In each situation the plan was the same. Keep up on technology, update and upgrade systems when necessary, fix things that break and do what you can to keep them from breaking again. But the most important of all, keep systems secure from malicious attacks.

Keep in mind when you are setting things up, that there is no right way and no single way to secure your stuff. Everyone and their dog will sell you something or let you download something to keep your knickers straight. You can go and drop hundreds of dollars for the best home router money can buy, get it home, turn it on and be surfing the Internet at speeds you never dreamed possible. Unfortunately you forgot to set an administrator password and a WPA security key. But don't worry, your neighbor didn't forget and he now has unrestricted access to your bandwidth, your network, your PC and everything you do on it.

I know, I know, you didn't forget to set the password on your new router and you even setup WPA so all your wireless traffic is secure, right? Except your kid just went to his or her favorite gaming site and it was infected with a Trojan that exploits a Flash vulnerability and guess what, you just got owned. Perhaps your wife received an email from her uncle in Sudan with an attachment of his vacation pictures to England and BAM! You just got infected with a bot, and are now part of a Spammers network. The scenarios can go on and on. You are probably thinking that it is just so much work to keep things secure, up to date, and safe from the outsiders that you shouldn't even try. Perhaps you are thinking it is just too expensive. But don't worry it is easy; it can be done in an afternoon; and I will show you step by step how easy it is. I will even tell you some easy rules to live by so you can make sure you don't leave any doors open.

You may have noticed that this book is not that long. This is something I have stewed over for some time. The truth is, I could make it a lot longer but one thing I hate about technical books is that they are just too damn detailed! They usually include so much information that by time you have read a chapter, you want to put the thing down, burn it and never open it again. So to help you avoid any arson charges, I have done my best to keep it short, simple and easy to read. I assume you know what the Internet and other basic terms are, so I have not taken the time to explain them to you. If it is beneficial for you to learn more about a tool or program mentioned in the book I will include links that you can reference so you can learn more about it.

Contrary to what you may be thinking, I am human and I am restricted by the amount of time in a day so I am not familiar with *every* tool out there so if you know of some great tools that are not mentioned in this book I would love to hear about them so shoot me an email.

"93% of boys and 62% of girls are exposed to Internet porn before the age of 18." **

RULE NUMBER 1
SECURE YOUR BORDER

Secure my border? What the hell is this guy talking about? Right! Well I am not talking about making sure no one is sneaking across your lawn and through your teenage daughter's window. What I am talking about is any part of your electronic communication that is not under your control.

For example, I cannot control what Google, Yahoo, Bing, or Ask include in their search results, I also cannot control if my geek neighbors 6 year old son is trying to connect to my home computer to see what my tax documents contain. I can, however, determine what search results from Google or Yahoo are accessible, just like I can control whether my geek neighbors kids can get to my home computer or not. Don't worry; I am going to show you how you can control and minimize these kinds of risks. All for as little as possible. Remember, this is a book about doing things "On the Cheap." Right?

Let us assume you just bought an awesome high end router with all its bells and whistles, hooked it up to your ISP's cable or DSL Modem and now you are up and running. Your border now becomes anything past the connection between your wireless router and the Internet Service Provider, ISP, Carrier or just Provider, if you prefer. Don't forget to set an administrative password on the router! If you can, you should also change the login name. If you need help, refer to the quick setup guide that came with your router. It should tell you how to make any of the changes. Now, how do you keep your geek neighbor out? Well, whatever router you go with, make sure that you turn on its firewall, and enable every firewall feature available. If you run into trouble, you may need to scale it back, but at least you are using every blocking feature it provides to keep out your nosy neighbors. It is also a great idea to watch for any firmware updates from the vendor, firmware and other releases. This will resolve issues where there has been a security or other vulnerability, as well as issues with how the router handles different features.

When you setup the router, it is also best to disable any services, and features that you don't need. For example, there is probably a feature to disable IPsec. This is a technology for some office stiff, or IT geek to connect to their work computer so they can work from home. Who does that, right!? But if you are an average Internet user who just wants to check out the latest cat video on YouTube, update your Facebook status or stream videos on Netflix, then go ahead and disable this feature. Remember I am not saying that IPsec is bad, I am only saying you should disable every feature, port, or service that you are not using. That way if there is a vulnerability in IPsec, it will not affect you.

Let's talk about how to keep from accessing those inappropriate search results and other websites. Sure you can purchase services from your ISP. It usually only costs a small monthly fee, but you will be subject to what sites they label as inappropriate. In some cases you can even pay a larger monthly fee to have some customization. But there you go again, feeding the pockets of the ISP and not saving up for the new Corvette you have always dreamed of. OK, smart ass, what can I do then? Well a better, free solution is to setup your network to use OpenDNS. OpenDNS is a service that resolves hostnames. It keeps a database of these hostnames and categorizes them based on their content. When you setup your account you tell OpenDNS what categories of content are not allowed. Then when someone goes to say bomb.com, and you are blocking the Weapons category, or sex.com and you are blocking the Pornography category, they will be presented with a Blocked Site page similar to the following:

 Sorry, but sex.com is blocked on this network.

This site was categorized in: Adult Themes, Lingerie/Bikini, Sexuality, Nudity, Pornography

Contact your network administrator

The blocked page is customizable so you are not stuck with the default one provided that I included above. There are also paid versions of OpenDNS, that allow for a bit more customization you can implement if you so desire. On their site they have detailed information on the features of each option, but for basic blocking of site categories, the free one will work just fine for you.

Let's get started and setup OpenDNS for your network!

First off, connect to your awesome router and set it to use OpenDNS to resolve hostnames and give your network clients (*your home computers*) this same setting when they join your network. Even if you decide to not use OpenDNS for filtering, you can still use them to resolve hostnames for your network, and I would highly recommend it. Each router is different, but to set it to use OpenDNS, find the network settings page and enter the following IP Addresses for your DNS server settings:

208.67.222.222 and 208.67.220.220

These simply point to the OpenDNS servers for hostname resolution, you can enter any address first, as they are interchangeable.

You can see that I have entered the addresses into my router's configuration:

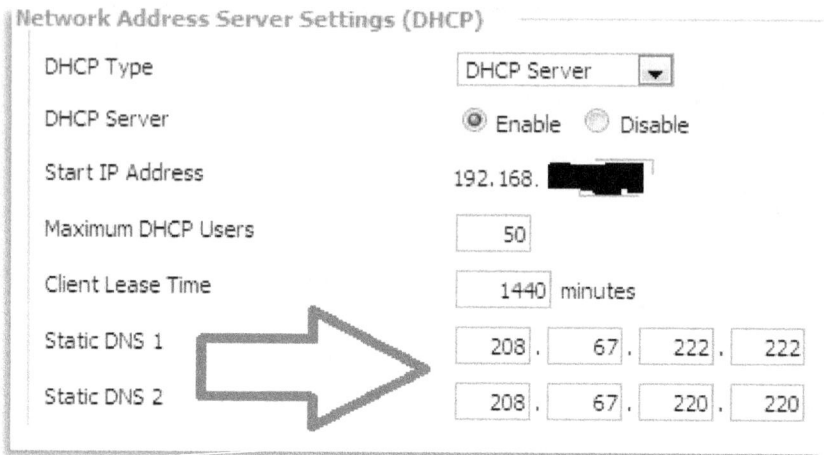

The above settings will setup my DHCP (PCs attached to my network, to use OpenDNS) it is also a great idea to set the router itself to use OpenDNS, so look through the settings on the router and make sure they all point to OpenDNS by entering the IP addresses I listed earlier. Some routers have multiple locations for setting DNS, one for DHCP clients, another for the router itself, be sure to set them all.

Now let's go to www.whatismyip.com and find out what your Public IP is. It will be listed at the top of the page:

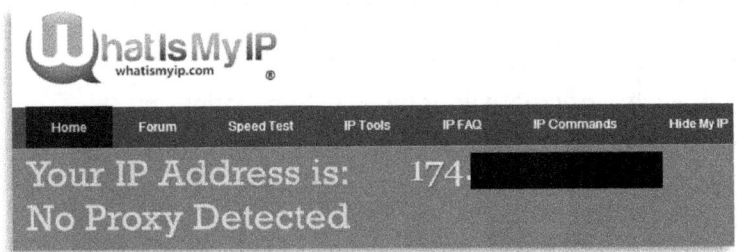

My public IP address is 174.X.X.X write yours down, because you will need it when we setup your OpenDNS account and configure a network. (I have used X.X.X, but you will have actual numbers)

Now that we have all the information we need, let's setup your OpenDNS account.

Navigate to https://www.opendns.com/home-solutions/parental-controls/ there are a few options you can choose from so choose whatever option is best to fit your needs. I will cover the OpenDNS Home option as it is Free and Customizable. However $19.95 per year for the OpenDNS Home VIP option is still a great bargain, and you just may get butterflies knowing you are helping an awesome solution remain free.

Once your account is setup, sign in and go to the "Settings" tab at the top. Now add your network by selecting the option, give it a name, and enter the IP Address you wrote down earlier.

Now click on the IP address and setup the filtering you want. You can choose 4 filtering options, as well as a completely custom option. Select the one you feel comfortable with, or create your own custom settings by blocking the site categories you want to keep off of your network.

Choose your filtering level

○	**High**	Protects against all adult-related sites, illegal activity, social networking sites, video sharing sites, and general time-wasters. 26 categories in this group - View - Customize
○	**Moderate**	Protects against all adult-related sites and illegal activity. 13 categories in this group - View - Customize
○	**Low**	Protects against pornography. 4 categories in this group - View - Customize
○	**None**	Nothing blocked.
◉	**Custom**	Choose the categories you want to block.

Once you have it setup, don't forget to apply your changes.

(APPLY)

Settings saved. Allow 3 minutes for your preferences to be pushed to all the servers.

You should have everything setup now and blocking should work for the categories you have selected to block. However, you will most likely need to reboot your pc, so you can get the new DNS settings applied to your computer when it tries to resolve host names. Since you have to wait 3 minutes for the changes to be applied, go ahead and reboot.

Now there is one other thing I want to mention. The IP address we wrote down earlier, depending on your ISP, this address can change from time to time. I have found that it changes very often when you have a DSL connection, and not very often when you have a Cable Internet connection. It really depends on your provider. So you will need to pay attention, if your blocking works fine one day and then not another, most likely your IP has changed and you need to update it. To do so, go to www.whatismyip.com to determine your new IP address, then go to OpenDNS.com, log into your account and make the changes.

OpenDNS has provided information on how to address locations where the IP address regularly changes. These types of changes are called Dynamic IP and are very common. So to assist you in making the process easier to update your changing IP, OpenDNS has created an OpenDNS Updater application. Go to the following OpenDNS page:

http://www.opendns.com/support/dynamic_ip_windows/

Then follow the instructions to download and install a dynamic IP updater client. Their instructions and detail are great, so I will not include them here.

"11: The average age of first exposure to Internet pornography." **

RULE NUMBER 2
SECURE YOUR NETWORK

Router

All right, now that we are keeping your kids from accessing Debbie's Double Dee's online, we can now get down to the business of making sure your network is secure. Networks come in all shapes and sizes but the basic fundamental aspects remain. There is a router that controls sending traffic to and from your network to the World Wide Web. There is a switch which connects your PCs to the router and a wireless device that does the same for your non-wired devices. And there is a firewall that should keep unwanted quests from accessing your tax files. For most home users, and most likely for you as well, these three devices will be the same device.

There are many different types of home routers you can get, each one will boast different features and have different bells and whistles. There are some good brands and bad ones, but depending on what you are looking for and how comfortable you are with some of the advanced features, get the one you like best that fits in your budget and looks cool. I mean what the heck is a router good for if it does not look cool, right? Don't forget to read some user reviews as well. You will probably get some good "geek" reviews to help you pick out a good one.

When you are looking for a router I would suggest that you find one that has the features you are looking for and that will provide the most Bang for your buck! Remember, everyday new technologies are created and new standards are approved so you will never get ALL the bells and whistles, because even though the feature may be announced it may not be available yet. I would recommend that the router you get includes at least the following features:

Needed Features:

802.11N
Security Encryption
Guest Access
Backup and Restore
Network Address Translation (NAT)
Quality of Service
IPv6 Enabled

Nice to have Features:

Gigabit Ports
USB Storage
MAC Address Filtering
Port Forwarding
VPN Pass through
Dynamic DNS (DDNS)

Hopefully you already did this, but take a moment to log into your router, change the administrator name from admin to something else like boogie man or chimp or anything but admin. Then change the password from, yup you guessed it, admin or password, (these are usually the passwords set by the manufacturer) and make it something hard to guess. 12345, password, God, sex among others are not good passwords. Your password should be at least 6 to 8 characters and include upper and lower case letters, numbers and symbols. There are hundreds of different approaches to passwords, and if you search online you are going to find that anything you use is not secure enough and that it will eventually get hacked, so pick something you are comfortable with and plan on changing it regularly. Be sure and write it down, memorize it or something so you don't forget it when you need it later. Don't worry I will cover a great password vault software for you later and tell you what you need to keep your passwords safe and available.

For those of you who feel adventurous there are a few open source router projects out there that can modify your $60 router's software so that it has extra features and performs more like a $300 router. These projects allow you to look up your router and download a version of software for it. Not all routers are supported, but if yours is on the list, I suggest you do some research and root your router so that you can take advantage of these features. Links to the projects are listed below:

DD-WRT: http://www1.k9webprotection.com/get-k9-web-protection-free

TOMATO: http://www.polarcloud.com/tomato

"Treat your password like your toothbrush. Don't let anyone else use it, and get a new one every six months." – Clifford Stoll

---

RULE NUMBER 3
SECURE YOUR PC

YAY, the Rule you have been waiting for. How in the world am I going to secure my PC? Well don't worry, with a few free tools and some diligence it is not going to be too hard. But for starters you need to make sure it is UP TO DATE! Yup, the number one cause of PC infection is because you are running an out of date software application; it just got exploited and you are now giving all your bank information to a guy in Somalia. Thankfully, though, there are some awesome companies with awesome products that will help you know when you have an out of date application. Just for your information, recently Java and Adobe have been releasing update after update to patch holes, and fix security issues, so keep an eye on those two.

The best way to know if you have up to date software is to use a little tool called "Secunia PSI". This is a free tool for the home user/consumer that will scan your pc and notify you of any out of date software. It will even give you links to update the software for easy download, or, in some cases it will run the patch with your approval. To download and install this awesome little gem, open your browser and go to http://secunia.com.

On the right side of the page is a blue link that says "Free Download" it is located under the "Secunia PSI" section. On the next page that opens just click the green download button. Once downloaded install the application on your PC.

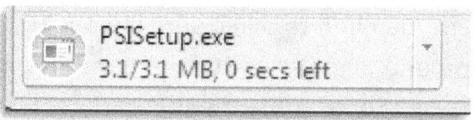 The application is easy enough to use so I will not include detailed instructions on the installation and usage of this application. Keep in mind it is only available for Windows systems and I mention it because it is a great tool to install on your Windows PC that is free, and easy to use. Here is what the scan progress screen will look like.

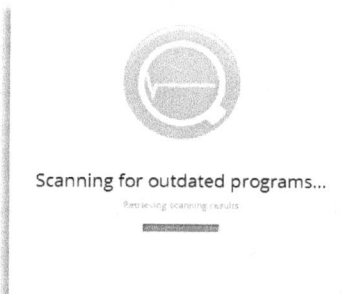

You can also see that after my initial scan on my test system, that I have some updating to do. Whats that! Adobe Reader needs an update? Theres a surprise for you.

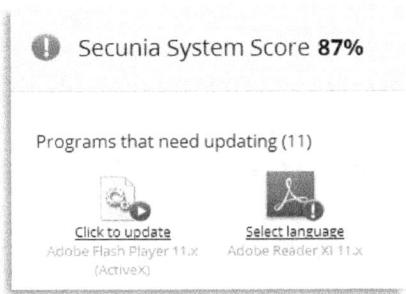

Once you get here you are much better off!

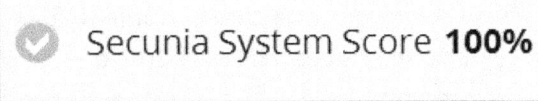

Anti-Virus

It is up to you how you want to update any software either manually or automatically so you decide what option is best for you.

Whoops we forgot about Anti-Virus, dang I was hoping you would forget so I could still send you all those wonderful email attachments. AV is a necessary evil, some argue that the whole AV thought process is out dated and needs to be changed entirely. They are probably right, but it has not changed yet and still needs to be addressed.

There are multiple options both free and non-free versions of anti-virus, each has its pros and cons and each claims its superiority over the other. Symantec, McAfee, Sophons and Kaspersky have been around for a long time, Avast, ClamWin, AVG and others are newer. Some solutions will eat up all your prcocessing speeds and others will take forever to download updates. Some are very manual, some are all automated. But what one is the best one?

I know my next suggestion may raise eyebrows and cause controversy between AV vendors and proponents, but keep in mind I am writing this book with the idea that there are ways to keep you secure at home with spending little to no cash. So here goes; choose a free one. Yup it's that simple. I have used nearly all of the above mentioned solutions and have found that the free ones work just as good. To be honest, there are things I don't like about all of them. So I have a hard time spelling out which one to get. But, if I was to suggest one, I would suggest that you download and install Microsoft Security Essentials. It is free, easy to use and does just as good as any other free and non-free versions available. But if you like another option better, than go with that one. The bottom line is that there are good free options available so you don't need to spend 30 or more dollars a year on somehting that is readily available and does the job.

Passwords

Ahh the wonderful password delema. How to choose a good, safe, secure and easy to remember password.

> It would take a desktop PC about
> **0.000004394 seconds**
> to crack your password

Well it is not easy, and a magic password does not exist. Any password you create or use can eventually be hacked, cracked, broke, choked, used and abused. If you don't believe me go to this site and check out how secure your password is:

https://howsecureismypassword.net/

The important thing to keep in mind is, you still have to use one, and you don't want to forget it. So now what? Where do you write it down, and when do you change it. This answer might surprise you. Don't write it down and don't remember it. Create it, set it, and forget it. Don't be shocked, by this answer, there are tools available online and downloadable that can help you with your passwords.

> It would take a desktop PC about
> # 6 decillion years
> to crack your password

A few of the tools you can use are LastPass, Roboform, KeePass, SplashID and 1Password. These are all great tools so you can choose one that makes sense for you. If you go to our friends at Lifehacker.com they have a great article on all five that can help you decide which one to use, just go to http://lifehacker.com/5529133/five-best-password-managers .

I recommend that you download and use KeePass (http://keepass.info/). I like this one because it keeps a locally encrypted database with all your passwords and other

KeePass
Password Safe

information. You can attach files etc. to the database and be assured that it is safe. All you have to do is decide on a Master Password that you will use to open it. Make sure it is not something you use on any of your websites, and make sure it is something secure. You can also use it to generate passwords that are secure and it will tell you how secure they are. There is plenty of information on their website to help you get acquainted with the product so I will not cover any of that here.

Browsers

Yuck, which browser to use? I do have an opinion and a preference here and I will try not to be too overbearing. In a corporate setting, I never install any browser that does not come native with the Servers Operating System. For home users, I think that you need to choose the one that gives you the best online experience. I will tell you however that I do like the customization of Chrome and Firefox. You can add extensions and applications that will enhance your online experience as well as keep you safe from certain online threats.

Between the two, I would recommend Google's Chrome browser. The ease of use is much better than Firefox and it is nicer looking. Just like with Firefox, you can have all your backgrounds and other image customizable options. So to enhance your online security, I would highly recommend using Chrome and install the following extensions:

 **DoNotTrackMe**
★★★★★ (1619) Productivity

 **Poper Blocker**
★★★★✦ (125) Productivity

 **WebFilter Pro - The best filtering addon!**
from www.cloudacl.com
WebFilter Pro is cloud based web filtering application protectin, monitoring millions web sites

To install extensions in Chrome, click the Settings button located in the upper right of the Chrome window.

Then select the "Settings" option near the bottom of the menu. From the settings window, select the "Extensions" menu and then "Get more extensions".

From This page click on the "Get more extensions" link at the bottom and then search for the extensions I have mentioned.

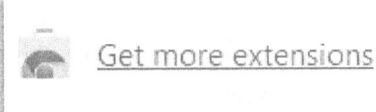

I also suggest you look through the available extensions to implement any that you think will give you a better online experience.

If you decide to use Firefox, similar and possibly the same extensions are available so install them for that browser as well. For Internet Explorer users, extensions are called "Add-Ons" and you will need to search for similar add-ons for this browser.

Web Filtering

     I know I have covered how to web filter on the Network side with RULE NUMBER 1 by using OpenDNS. I have also mentioned using the "WebFilter Pro" extension in Chrome in this RULE NUMBER 3. Both of these options are great and you definitely want to use them. You will find that the web blocking is customizable for each one, and you can be as restrictive as you like or not as restrictive as you like. However, I have found that inappropriate images or other items will still be available inside of search results if you only use the two above mentioned solutions.

     For example if you don't block search engines with OpenDNS or WebFilter Pro, but you do block pornography, when you search for pornographic images or content, you cannot force Safe Searching on the search engine, and you cannot block the image results in the browser. If you click on the search result image or link the page will be blocked. But for a teenager exploring his unedited sexuality, that thumbnail image of Carmen Electra, is probably enough to understand the Birds and the Bees.

Web Access Blocked

You can take multiple approaches on how to set it up, be really restrictive on the browser filtering and not so much on OpenDNS, or vice versa. What I recommend is that you restrict with OpenDNS everything you do not want anyone on your network to access, then use the WebFilter Pro to restrict further those sites that you do not want your children from accessing.

I know what you are thinking, "What if they use Internet Explorer or another browser that does not have the WebFilter Pro extension?" You still want to restrict your family from going to sites that are inappropriate. If this is the case, then I recommend you register for your free copy of a little Web Filter Gem called "K9 Web Filter". This is basically an application that you install on your PC, setup an administrative password, setup restrictions and it works on the back end so that any browser you use is restricted by the defined policies.

You can register and download for a free copy of K9 by going to their web site which can be found at the following link:

http://www1.k9webprotection.com/get-k9-web-protection-free.

You are required to register to get a license key, but it is wholly worth it. Their web site has excellent information on how to setup and use the product so I will not include any detailed information on how to set it up in this book.

Now you're asking yourself, why do I need to use Web Filter Pro if I am just going to use the K9 solution? The truth is, you don't need to. I have just included both options so you are aware they exist and can choose the best option for your situation. Then why do I need to use OpenDNS if I use K9 for filtering, simple, because you have devices connecting to your network that cannot run K9, therefore you need to stop them from accessing those inappropriate and malicious sites as well.

"40 million U.S. adults regularly visit Internet pornography websites, and 10% of adults admit to Internet sexual addiction." – Internet Filter Review, 2006. **

RULE NUMBER 4
SECURE YOUR MOBILE DEVICES

If you have made it this far and implemented my suggestions then you are doing great, your home network is as secure as it can be and you are keeping hackers, spammers and bot netters away. Good Job. But you are not done yet. Your android, your iPhone, your Kindle, your nook and other mobile devices that you own also need to be secured.

If you have chosen to implement OpenDNS, then you can be sure that the devices are safe from malicious code and inappropriate web site access while on your network. But you should also take care to ensure that they are safe when on the mobile networks. For your android and iPhone mobile devices I suggest at a minimum you install "Sophos Security and Antivirus" or "Lookout Security & Antivirus". Both are free and provide excellent features to keep your mobile devices secure from online threats.

Whenever you install a new application be mindful of what it requires access to. A flashlight application that wants to have cell phone, or data storage access, may not be a legitimate application. You should also put a password on your phone. I don't care if it is a 4 digit password, a swipe word, pattern or whatever your device supports, but for gosh sakes put a dang password on your phone. Sure there are exploits you can find on the Internet, but if you don't have a password set, then you are just asking for someone to steal your phone and your stuff.

Be careful when going to suspicious links from a web site or email, and be very careful whenever you are using an unknown Wi-Fi hot spot. What do I mean when I say be careful? Well for starters, don't open your Chase or other Bank or financial institutions application to check your balances or transfer money when you are connected to any Wi-Fi hotspot other than one you know where it originated from. This type of activity will only increase your possibility of identity theft and fraud.

I also suggest setting up encryption of your mobile devices data. If your device supports encryption, it is easy to setup and will give you much better peace of mind if you happen to lose your phone or it gets stolen.

Mobile phone browsing

Something we need to look at is mobile phone browsers. We know when we are at home that inappropriate sites are not accessible because we configured and are using OpenDNS for all our wireless devices. But, what happens when the device is at a friend's house or on the mobile network? Well unfortunately there is no great answer. I have searched and used a dozen filter apps for android and iPhone and have yet to find one that works flawlessly or at least at the same level as OpenDNS does.

Thankfully however, K9 has recently released an Android version of their filter and the Web Filter Pro Extension you are using in Chrome, has an Android and iPhone version as well. It is called "Cloudacl". You will find however that these products have a wide range of good and bad reviews and you may just want to try each one to get your own taste of their functionality and decide which is best. My next suggestion would be to keep your eye on these two solutions as I believe they are just going to be getting better.

"34% of Internet users have experienced unwanted exposure to porn either through pop up ads, misdirected links or emails"

RULE NUMBER 5
STAY VIGILANT

What do I mean by stay vigilant? Well I mean just that. Remember that if someone wants to hack your data, they are going to try. Your job is to make it hard so that they will move on to the next guy and take his instead. That being said, I decided to put in this last rule to give you a few ideas on how to be vigilant with your security.

Email

No matter how good it sounds and how awesome it would be, you DO NOT, have any relatives or any blood line to some huge or large amount of money in another country. You will never get it, you will never see it and even if you try to get some from the bank, you will be a SUCKER if you try.

Passwords

Remember use different passwords for every site you use, keep track of them with KeePass and whenever one of your sites is exploited, change the password associated with that site, you will not need to change the others because they don't match. Also do not use easily guessed or simple passwords. Use something with letters, symbols, and numbers.

DO NOT ever give your password to anyone, including your IT guy. They don't want to have the liability of knowing it and a good IT guy should never ask for it anyway.

If you do give them your password, when they are done doing whatever, change it and change it fast.

Personal Information

NEVER EVER give out your personal information to anyone who calls you or asks you via email. Personal information includes passwords, credit card numbers, account numbers, social security numbers, waist size, blood type, hair color, etc. No one really needs this unless you are calling them to pay a bill or verify something with the business entity. If you make the call it is okay. If they call you, get their name and number, hang up. Look up the real number online. Call it back and ask for that person. You may be just making it hard on yourself and over doing it, but it is better safe than sorry.

Two Factor Authentication

Some online services are starting to allow for two factor authentication. This usually requires a registered cell phone that can receive a txt message or call to determine that it is indeed you trying to access the account. I would highly recommend using two factor authentication for any online services you use.

Browser Passwords

Most browsers will prompt you to save the passwords you enter to log into sites. This functionality is a great feature and will enhance your online experience. Whether you do or do not take advantage of these features is up to you, but IE and Chrome have some excellent measures to keep your passwords safe:

> Here is a great article on what Chrome does to secure your passwords:
> http://www.howtogeek.com/70146/how-secure-are-your-saved-chrome-browser-passwords/
>
> Here is a great article on what Internet Explorer does to secure your passwords:
> http://www.howtogeek.com/68231/how-secure-are-your-saved-internet-explorer-passwords/

Keeping Kids Safe

Let's be honest. We all know there is a lot of crap on the Internet that we do not want to subject our kids to. When they are older we can let them make their own decisions, but as parents, we should ensure that each session our kids have on the Internet should be a positive one. To help ensure our kids safety there are some free solutions out there. OpenDNS, K9 and others I have mentioned are great for keeping this safe, but for additional monitoring there are a few free options:

Norton Family: This is a free service that helps protect your kids when they go online. You can monitor time limits, social network, Internet Searches and more. There is a free version and Premier version with more advanced features and is definitely a product to check out.

https://onlinefamily.norton.com/familysafety/basicpremium.fs

uknowkids.com: Is a service similar to Norton family. It does not have all the features that the Norton Family free version does, but it also has a few different versions to try and the basic one is free.

https://www.uknowkids.com/pricing-and-plans/

Minor Monitor: This is basically a free software that helps parents know what their kids are doing on Facebook, and alerts parents or allows parents to review the activity.

http://www.minormonitor.com/

There are probably hundreds of different solutions for monitoring your children online, but the best example and tool you have as a parent is to make sure your children know what is and what is not appropriate and make sure you live by the same mantra you are asking them to live by.

You can have a positive online experience and you can keep your computer, your kids, and your family safe from online threats by following the five rules I have listed in this book. Now go out there, enjoy what the Internet has to offer.

"56% of divorces involve one spouse's continued use of Internet pornography" – Family Research Council, The Effects of Pornography, 2009

APPENDIX

Helpful links and information that you can use to help you become familiar with the items contained in this book. Some of these links can also be found in the text of this book.

OpenDNS: The World's Largest Internet Security Network
http://www.opendns.com/

DD-WRT: The free Linux-based firmware for several wireless routers. http://www1.k9webprotection.com/get-k9-web-protection-free

Tomato: a small, lean and simple replacement firmware for Linksys, Buffalo and other Broadcom-based routers.
http://www.polarcloud.com/tomato

Secunia: Market leaders in computer security software and research.
http://secunia.com/

KeePass: The free, open source, light-weight and easy-to-use password manager.
http://keepass.info/

LastPass: The Last password you'll have to remember.
https://lastpass.com/

Roboform: A top-rated password manager and web from filler.
http://www.roboform.com/

SplashID: Secure password management for iPhone, iPad, Android
http://www.splashdata.com/splashid/

1Password: Have you ever forgotten a password?
https://agilebits.com/onepassword

K9 Web Protection: What do you want to protect?
http://www1.k9webprotection.com/

Sophos Naked Security Blog: News, Opinion, advice and research from Sophos.
http://nakedsecurity.sophos.com/

**: Pornography statistics
http://purehope.net/resources/statistics/
http://unitedfamiliesinternational.wordpress.com/2010/06/02/14-shocking-pornography-statistics/

"Only 23 percent of parents have rules about what their kids can do on the computer." **

Glossary

I know I said I wouldn't explain the terms to keep the book short. But for those that really want to know here are a few definitions.

Router: A small physical device that joins multiple networks together

ISP: Internet Service Provider, ISP is a company that supplies Internet connectivity to home and business customers.

Nosy Neighbor: That guy or girl that just seems to know everything about everyone and can usually be found on the phone relaying that information.

Firewall: A system designed to prevent unauthorized access to or from a private network.

Geek: Short for *computer geek,* an individual with a passion for computers, to the exclusion of other normal human interests.

Office Stiff: That guy or girl that is there before anyone and leaves after everyone. They often go on vacation only to work remotely from their laptop while on the beach.

Hostname: A label that is assigned to a device connected to a computer network and that is used to identify the device in various forms of electronic communication such as the World Wide Web or e-mail.

IP Address: An identifier for a computer or device on a TCP/IP network.

DHCP Client: A computer system that receives is Internet Protocol (IP) address from a central server.

"12% of the websites on the Internet are pornographic, that's over 24 Million sites." **

About the Author

Lance is an IT Veteran with nearly 15 years of IT experience and has enjoyed nearly every minute of it. He does not consider himself a geek, not that there is anything wrong with that, but loves Marvel Comic movies and believes he is the inspiration behind "The Wolverine" except for the muscle, Adamantium, attitude and hair. He loves to learn new technologies and embraces the thought that anything can be done right on a small budget. He enjoys backpacking, sports, and hanging out with his wife and kids.

You can contact Lance via email at info@nsenetworks.com

www.ingramcontent.com/pod-product-compliance
Lightning Source LLC
Chambersburg PA
CBHW072302170526
45158CB00003BA/1154